JACQUELINE PIRTLE

Truth BE told

An inner journey

I dedicate this journal to ALL teenagers in the universe.

You are our future, making the world a better place, and for that I thank you from the "sane" of my brain.

praise for jacqueline

"I love Jacqueline's books. They are great for adults and kids. We all have an inner genie and Jacqueline is teaching us how to hold on to it."

— Longtime Client and Reader

"Jacqueline's books are magickal teaching kids and adults how to listen to their intuition, emotions, and feelings."

— Longtime Client and Reader

"I love that Jacqueline Pirtle has written books about intuition that encourages youngsters and adults to listen to their inner voice and be who they came to be. I also love that she encourages parents to respect and allow their children to follow their inner genie, honor their auras when making decisions, and help them realize that they possess infinite wisdom and can learn how to tap into it. This is vital to a child's growth and development, yet I've never seen children books with these subject matters before. So, for that, I give Pirtle big kudos."

— Longtime Client and Reader

ISBN-13: 978-1-955059-73-2

Publisher: Jacqueline Pirtle - Freaky Healer

Editor-in-chief: Zoe Pirtle

Book cover design by Kingwood Creations kingwoodcreations.com

Author photo courtesy of Lionel Madiou madious.com

Dear parent and caregiver,

As a holistic practitioner, energetic living expert, and emotional intelligence teacher I have written over 18 books for adults and children supporting people to live a more conscious, mindful, and happier life.

You can find out more at:
www.freakyhealer.com
Amazon Author Page

Hope you'll take a look!

Happiest,
Jacqueline

claim it!

This journal belongs to:

_____

_____

What's your happy place?
Go there, stay there, and never leave!

Hey teen star!

In your own detailed ways, tell me what it's like to be you in these times? How does it feel to be your age—is it hard, okay, or easy?

Do you know how powerful you actually are, but 'will be' even more so after working through this journal, understanding yourself and the world in the most clearest way ever?

To support this success in your life-endeavor and get you to your most fearless state I want to teach you about a technique I call, "Energetic Profiling."

Most will raise an eyebrow just reading this, but I count on you to give this a try by staying open in your heart, mind, ears, and eyes.

So here we go…

Imagine that you are energy and that all your energy has information stored inside of it. Your job is to sense that energy and translate what you sense into thoughts, then words, which create feelings to let you know how you feel—good or bad. Good feelings signal that you are living according to your true reasons of why you are here on earth, as your physical body, whereas bad feelings mean that you are not aligned with yourself fully and completely.

This journal is your roadmap to figuring out your energy and discovering yourself to create your own Energetic Profile.

By following the guidance in this journal and answering these deep questions you will write an artful piece about yourself while also stepping fully into the truth of who you really are, why you are alive and here, and what this all means to begin with.

Yes, you heard right! I want you to imagine that all your findings will be in article, column, report, or simple list style and make up the greatest piece of literature of all time. A masterpiece of a newspaper, all about you!

Why is this a big deal? Because you will write your heart out about YOU—one of the most important people representing our grand future. Powerful stuff, I know!

So, self-assessing teenager, are you ready to own your gifts and then maybe, possibly, and probably share your wisdom with other people in the world?

I sure hope you say yes, because in some sure way I know that you have it in you to teach the whole universe about living a happy and fun life. Okay then, pressure's on, let's go!

And remember, you are a superstar!

Your biggest fan and fellow Energetic Profiler,

Jacqueline

(All of the above counts for parents, grandparents, and caretakers of young people too!)

P.S. At the end of this journal you will find some extra pages in case you turn into a writing machine and don't have enough space for all your results and findings—even for your urges to doodle or draw.

Go fill these pages up and have a blast!

DAY 1

Imagine you are hired to create a masterpiece of a newspaper - not just a column or half page but a full blown, page-by-page publication - about the most brilliant and interesting person there is.

But, there are two catches: 1) You only have 30 days to gather all the information, and 2) You're the one it's about, no-one else.

It might come as a shock to you, but you are our future and definitely categorize as brilliant and truly interesting.

Who you truly are, determining what you're made of and uncovering what you're all about is not only interesting, it's brilliant! Getting crystal clear on how you want to live your life is a skill; plus, there's no better outcome than finding yourself in the process, being closest to your truth than ever, all while claiming what fits, sorting out what doesn't, and honoring your gifts and how you enrich the world.

This is no small feat but I know you can do it. You have my full guidance and you have yourself, a trusted entity you can always count on.

So for today, breathe and let the fact that you are about to profile yourself sink in. Then describe how you feel before such an epic self-discovery; what outcome would you like? Tomorrow you'll start with pride and willingness but also excitement and curiosity.

_____

_____

_____

_____

DAY 2

Happy onboarding day! Let's fill out the necessities: write your full name - all of them - on the line below:

_____

How do you want others to pronounce your name(s)? If testing is needed, yell them into a pillow or shout them into a closet. Casually note down how you feel doing so:

_____

_____

To end your first day at the newspaper: write a little, covering how you feel about your name. What's special about your name, for you? Note down any insights on what your name mean to you —does it represent a certain mood, a color-tone, strength, power, fun, or anything else? Does your name point out specific talents? Short and sweet is fine, just make it count. Go...

_____

_____

_____

DAY 3

You mastered your journalistic day yesterday with charm!

Today, let's tackle your numbers to get more specific information for your paper. In case numerals are not your happiest thing ever don't worry, math isn't involved here—it's your birthday numbers you will scope out.

Write down your full birthdate:

_____

Now only look at your birth day number, the other ones will get your attention over the next few days.

How do you feel about your birth day number? Is there a touch of happiness, luckiness, strength, creativity, or intelligence attached to that number? Do you see a certain talent it represents?

Ready to think like a journalist? Get cracking, write a short feature about your unique birth day number:

_____

_____

_____

_____

_____

DAY 4

On a scale of 1-10, how much truth can be found in your personal numbers? Hint: a lot!

With your highest curiosity in place, write down your birth month number and study that number deeply for a minute or two.

_____

Then, close your eyes and take a deep breath to get yourself into a relaxed or meditative state. There, visualize and think of your birth month. Ask yourself: what's my meaning of it—does my month feel huge or tiny, powerful and strong, or something else?

When ready open your peakers with speed and write a short write-up about your birth month.

_____

_____

_____

_____

_____

_____

_____

DAY 5

What's big and is yours? Your birth year number!

Go ahead, shake out your doubts and life's traps, empty your mind and open your heart, then jot down your birth year number. Stare at it like you mean it!

_____

Ready to close your eyes and take a nap?

Just kidding! Stay with me here, breathe and hone in on your expectation of finding out a great deal about your big number.

Questions to ask are: What's my meaning of my birth year? What do I feel, see, hear, and think of my birth year? Is there a specific force in that year, or something big that happened in my year? Research if you must.

All insights count, even the ones that don't make sense or are faint. Trust them, and start your report to make your newspaper of the interesting sort!

_____

_____

_____

_____

_____

DAY 6

Who doesn't like a good party?!

Imagine today's your birthday! Just go with it. Next, visualize the most mouthwatering cake you have ever seen—it's big and gorgeous, deliciously smelling, perfect and just the way you like it. Coolest fact: it's all yours.

Tell me, what type of cake is it? I want to know the flavor, size, form, color, everything—but also, how many candles there are. Meaning, what is your real age today?

_____

_____

Next, stare down your age until you win and have what you want: information and details you seek.

How do you feel being that old, what's your vibe; powerful, agitated, excited, or a feeling of being free, alive, pushed into a mold? Also, what energy does your age carry? Feeing silly? Then ask your age how it would dress to impress—if it could. Then ready, set for a few great sentences:

_____

_____

_____

DAY 7

Psst, time to dive into your timely secrets and write a great story!

What time were you born? Ask around if needed because there's no skipping this clarity. Go ahead, write down your special hour and minute, then focus *a lot* on these numerals:

_____

Once you are sure that you can see the imprint of your birth hour even through the dark of your eyelids, you can close your eyes. Ask yourself what energy was present when your arrival was in action. What meaning does your birth hour carry—what are the specifics of the hour you started being you?

_____

_____

Onward to your minute; see the number in your mind's eye, and then go dark. How do you feel about this blink of an eye moment? What does this timing mean for you?

_____

_____

DAY 8

Hard to believe you were once tiny as a tot, isn't it? However, facts show that once upon a time baby you was born. But where? Go ahead, write down your birth place:

_____

What's your first thought about your birth place—do you like it?

_____

Next let's hear your second, but only after reading this: the 'where' that you first peeked the light of day in is your special place, and not by coincidence. Your birth place is yours and holds immense truth about who you really are.

Close your eyes, see if you can visualize how it looked *where* and *when* you were born. What's coming in; a feeling, thought, noise, sound, or sign? Time to write your "hello world" piece:

_____

_____

_____

_____

Let me blow your mind by saying "everything is energy; you too!"

It's a fact and proven: the smallest building block and foundation of everything and everyone is energy. We are made of energy and everything about life is always about energy. Everything we do, say, think, and feel is energy, but also when we breathe or walk, we are acting as energy—and energy is always new because that's how energy behaves; always moving and changing. Simply put we are walking clouds of energy, moving in life; energy.

Let's test that! Rate the energy you feel right now and give it a descriptive word:

_____

Second energetic investigation: Shift way back to when you took your first breath! Close your eyes, breathe deep, feel into that incredible moment. Focus and sense the special power your first filling of your lungs holds—you might even see colors, sparks, or light.

How did you feel back then? What force did you come into this world with—what energy did your first breath hold? Cool fact: that strong energy is yours to BE your whole life! Notes please:

_____

_____

_____

Are you crazy? Do you hear a voice inside yourself—at times in your head, heart, stomach, or everywhere?

No, you're not crazy. On the contrary, you couldn't be better since it's a normal part of being human. In fact, it's crucial not only that you are aware of it, but also listen to it, because this phenomenon is called your inner voice, intuition, or instinct. Your inner voice is an invisible power you have, it's always right, and it's unique to you—plus, it's energy.

Let's tackle your loudest inner words first; your head-voice. Tip: close your eyes for this one, it will help you hear it clearer.

Can you hear it? What is it saying? Don't be shy, ask it, "Do you hear me?" "What do you want to tell me?" "What do I need to know about myself?"

Jot down your answers here, to make a special statement in your journalism piece.

_____

_____

_____

_____

_____

_____

Put your hands on your heart and repeat after me:

"My heart knows best and always points me towards who I am, what I want, and what's right for me. It's where I feel my love, happiness, satisfaction, and all other good-feeling emotions."

To learn how to hear and feel the powerful guidance produced by your never resting love-engine, let's create your baseline first.

How big is your heart? How strongly are you experiencing love, joy, and happiness today? In gigantic, huge, big, medium, or small ways?

_____

Time to soul search! Close your eyes, breathe deep, and keep your hands on your heart. Feel it beating. Can you hear your heart's voice? Are you listening to what it has to say? Also ask: "What and how do I feel?" "What is my heart telling me?"

Go on, be cheesy, and write your own love story: you and your heart.

_____

_____

_____

_____

Hey inspired writer! Today is one of those dark days...

An investigation into the deep darkness of your stomach is in order. I'm told it's moonless and quiet there, and that its inner voice feels a lot like a deep inner knowing. Let's check if that's true.

Have you ever had a situation where you knew that something is for you, or not for you? Or seen a thing in a store full of things, knowing that this one thing has to be yours—or that without someone finishing their sentence you already knew your answer, or choice? Yes or no? What did that clear knowing feel like?

_____

_____

That's your gut intuition, a gut feeling, showing itself like a clear and deep inner knowing. To practice hearing and trusting it, close your eyes, place your hands on your stomach, and breath deeply.

Ask your gut-knowing: "What do I know?" "What am I certain of?" "What do I need to know?" "What do I want to know?" Time for the next set of inspiring notes:

_____

_____

_____

DAY 13

Take a huge deep breath, hold it, then let it go!

Can you feel the power of your oxygen-machine, your lungs? Note how they fill like air tanks with every breath in - charging you with powerful life-force - while every breath out helps cleanse out gunked up energy, making room for even more life to come in. How does it feel to fill up with such energy?

_____

_____

This day calls for you to get back to your first breath again. Remember, Day 9 already got you there. Need a quick revisit?

Close your eyes. Imagine being born right now, and that you are taking your very first breath. Let's go, inhale and make it count!

How does this first filling of your lungs feel? Strong, undeniable, unstoppable? Question: can every deep breath **now** still fill you with that same life-force, like your first breath did? Write, energized one, write...

_____

_____

_____

_____

"Why?" A word, and sentence, initiating inspiring thought processes while also bringing incredible answers to the news room by providing incredible clarity. I say, ask your "why's" a lot!

You are invited to go deep into your core to define your unique "why's." Like what's your big "why"—but also your little itty bitty "why's" that come with being you?

Take a deep breath, close your eyes, and put your laser-sharp focus on these questions: "What am I here on earth to do?" "What energy am I here to share?" "What is my job, besides being alive, living as a human being, and writing a newspaper about myself?"

Make this the paragraph of all time!

_____

_____

_____

_____

_____

_____

_____

_____

Let's assess your inspired side!

What are you unshakably passionate about? What is the thing that, when you follow it's calling, harmony is created in you and for you—but when going against, havoc nests in the entirety of your life? What would you give anything for because without, your life is literally over? What would you trade favorites for in order to do it, have it, or have the "it" happening—maybe even consider pushing forcefully against anything or anyone standing in your path or power to make it happen? When does your most powerful passion strike? Can this writing piece make the front page?

_____

_____

_____

_____

One more thing: how do you feel about such forceful passions and what is your experience when your passions are being denied?

_____

_____

_____

Pick 3 of your favorite material things. Go:

1._____

2._____

3._____

Then right behind the material item, write down the strongest purpose it has. Keep it short and don't think too hard. For example: My phone. Serves as a communication tool and more.

Now it's your turn! Get to the bottom of your strongest purpose, besides living your heroic life on this planet. What is it, and how are you using your purpose? Who are you helping with your purpose? How does your purpose make you feel?

Make it a strong piece for this print that's all about you:

_____

_____

_____

_____

_____

_____

Talent show! But not the boring kind.

List 2 close people that you consider superstars, then dig deep into the 'why' to find their talents. What's so impressing about them? Note it all down:

_____

_____

Time to point the finger at yourself, superstar! What are your talents, what impresses you about yourself? For an out of body experience, step outside yourself and look through the eyes of others; what do they see in you? List at least 5 of your incredible gifts! How do they make you feel? What are you doing with them? Go on, write your bestseller anecdote:

_____

_____

_____

_____

_____

_____

Delicate subject alert: What's love got to do with you?

Love has many facets and can be hurtful, but the butterfly side of it is real too and so are the waves of gratitude, happiness, fun, and smiles. Hard not to want more when it feels that good.

There are also multiple types of love: for loved ones, friends, partners, and pets; for things, activities, outings, fun times; for being lazy, sleeping, napping, and being silly. It's all love.

The most powerful love, however, is the one that nobody else but you can claim and feel; your love for yourself. What does self-love feel like? How do you practice it, and how do you measure how much you love yourself?

_____

_____

Next, pretend you have a body scanner. With it find where your love sits in your body; is it in your head, heart, or stomach? Are there traces in your legs, feet, arms, or hands? A sentence will do here:

_____

_____

_____

DAY 19

Armed with a sweet treat to balance possible sour-ness, let's tackle emotions today. Yes, they can get sour!

What are your strongest emotions you enjoy, how do they feel?

_____

_____

What are your strongest emotions you don't like or have trouble getting control of—how do they feel?

_____

_____

These tough feelings. What would be a good game plan or strategy when you feel them? For sure embrace them, but then what? How can you be proud of yourself to be able to feel that strongly and react in a way that is healthy for you?

_____

_____

_____

DAY 20

Brainpower! Trickiest thing ever.

Let's untrick it once and for all: the secret is to understand it clearly, then use it too your advantage. How do you feel about your brain? Are you using it loudly, proudly, and in clear alignment with who you are, or are you keeping it small and timid at times, not representing how intelligent you really are?

_____

_____

_____

If you could take a seat in your brain and look around with alert, what insights would you gain? How are things it in your noggin? What moods are present? Is there good energy available? What's the condition of your brain, is it all fired up? Most importantly, what is your brain telling you? Write your bain-iest report yet:

_____

_____

_____

_____

_____

Think you have a personal thought-race in your head? Good, because you do!

Your daily thousands of thoughts can solve everything or cancel all good feelings if not managed. They impact how you feel since thoughts create feelings, and depending on the quality of your thoughts - positive or negative - that is how you feel. Thoughts feed the mind either good or bad energy.

Want to know the real kicker? Your powerful mind likes to take over whenever it can, which is any time you are not fully focused in your now; thinking about yesterday, tomorrow, driving, doing schoolwork, hanging out with friends etc. Good news is, you can program your mind to be positive when thinking positively.

So when you think positive thoughts - feeding your mind good energy - how do you feel? What's your favorite thought coming from your heart?

_____

_____

To fully understand, how does your mind feel when you feed it negative or bad thoughts?

_____

_____

DAY 22

Everyone has wishes and dreams!

Even if you are convinced otherwise or don't know what those are, or could be, they are there and make up a pretty big chunk of who you are because every desire is unique to the one having it.

For today's piece of literature, ask yourself: "What are my deepest wishes and dreams?" "What would be cool to have, great to accomplish, or dreamy to experience?"

Don't forget to show some excitement and anticipation! Might even want to consider turning up the volume of awe for yourself and the complex goals you come up with.

Next, read every wish on your list, smile, and feel how good that desire and outcome feels to you. Then like you mean it say, "With gratitude, my wishes come true!" Voila, order placed, deal sealed.

Make your wishlist below.

_____

_____

_____

_____

_____

_____

_____

DAY 23

Let's trigger your "I feel so good" ways!

What's your happy place? How does your own personal adventure park in life, and for your age, look like? What brings you joy and gets you laughing until your legs are crossed because it's too late to run to the bathroom? What says "fun and crazy" to you? What are your coolest moments, who's involved, and what's the bliss all about?

Write your happy list, make it inspiring and contagious.

_____

_____

_____

_____

_____

_____

_____

_____

_____

_____

_____

DAY 24

Food is never just food since the what, when, how, and where differs for every single person. Plus, knowing your personal food-facts makes life more fun and easier because of how powerful it is to be able to communicate such core findings when a food situation arises. And they do!

What's your take on food? What's the meaning of food for you—what do you enjoy about food, and what do you not? What's your favorite way of eating; speed eating or taking forever, stuff it in hamster-style or delicate bites, on the go or seated? What about in company; eating in groups or does the smacking get to you hence, tucked away in a corner alone is best? What about the where; outside or inside, couch, floor, bed, or table? Lastly, what are the yummiest foods in the world and how do you feel when devouring them? What's a "yuck no," and why?

_____

_____

_____

_____

_____

_____

_____

_____

DAY 25

Every winner starts as a beginner!

Relax before you go hunting for information here. Let's be honest, your winner alignment might be off a bit since you drift into someone else's winner-line often, hiding what you think a 'winner who's winning' is.

So first close your eyes and breathe deeply; fill your oxygen tanks and feel how you are creating more life than you have ever experienced. Then breathe out and sense how you are making space for a whole lot of winner energy for what's to come.

When you feel relaxed, imagine the following winner scene: You being a winner, having a winner day, winning at whatever you are doing. You are a winner!

Feel yourself stepping into this winner clip. You ARE it. Feel this!

Next, answer the following questions like you're at an interview podium: How do you feel, being a winner? What are you doing, what is the winning experience you are having—what is winning for you? Are you smiling? What are you wearing? Do you feel strong and bold? Are you happy? Who is with you?

_____

_____

_____

_____

_____

Congrats! You managed the tough stuff just fine; on to some lighter yet newspaper worthy fact checking now:

Fact 1:

What should the world know about you? What do you want your friends and family to know about you? What are you proud of yourself for?

_____

_____

_____

_____

_____

_____

_____

_____

_____

_____

_____

DAY 27

Fact 2:

Imagine you can do whatever you want. What will that be, and how do you want to do it? Where will you do your favorite thing, and what will you *need* to do what you want to do?

_____

_____

_____

_____

_____

_____

_____

_____

_____

_____

_____

_____

_____

Fact 3:

You are a genius—an exceptional, intellectual, creative power, with your own natural ability.

What is it, and what does your genius look like to you? Is your genius outside or inside of you? How powerful is it? How can you use it to be a kind person and to help others?

_____

_____

_____

_____

_____

_____

_____

_____

_____

_____

_____

DAY 29

Fact 4:

Imagine you could choose your perfect life. How would you like your life to be? Where would you want to live? What does your life there look like?

_____

_____

_____

_____

_____

_____

_____

_____

_____

_____

_____

_____

Fact 5:

Imagine you get to give a gift (or maybe a few) to the world, to make it better and nicer. What would the gift, or gifts, be?

_____

_____

_____

_____

_____

_____

_____

_____

_____

_____

_____

_____

_____

bonus

Because hey, you don't want your self-search for your truth to end.

So keep on profiling journalist, there's still so much to find out about yourself!

Find 15 words that describe you perfectly:

_____

_____

_____

_____

_____

_____

_____

_____

_____

_____

_____

_____

_____

DAY 32

List 15 places that you love, love, love:

_____

_____

_____

_____

_____

_____

_____

_____

_____

_____

_____

_____

_____

_____

_____

DAY 33

Name 15 activities that make you happy:

_____

_____

_____

_____

_____

_____

_____

_____

_____

_____

_____

_____

_____

_____

_____

DAY 34

Come up with 15 ways to be kind:

_____

_____

_____

_____

_____

_____

_____

_____

_____

_____

_____

_____

_____

_____

_____

DAY 35

What makes the world a better place? Think of 15 ideas:

_____

_____

_____

_____

_____

_____

_____

_____

_____

_____

_____

_____

_____

_____

extra pages

How cool is it that you don't have to sweat the small stuff—like not having enough space for all your results and findings or to refrain from doodling or drawing?

Just come on over here and use these extra pages for whatever needs you have to scratch, and most importantly, have fun while you're at it.

Truth Be Told

Truth Be Told

Truth Be Told

thank you!

Let's be honest here... I have a dream team!

I could not have finished this book without the help of talented, creative, and phenomenal professionals and the guidance of ALL young people in my life.

From the bottom of my heart, I want to thank Zoe Pirtle for her editorial mastery; kingwoodcreations.com for their fun and polished book cover design; and madiouART.com for an amazing photo shoot.

I'd also like to extend a huge "Thank You!" to all fans of my work and books—I created this beautiful journal for ALL the young people in this universe.

Life is spectacular with teenagers on our side!

and last but not least

I truly hope you enjoyed this journal as much as I loved writing it, and if that's so, it would be wonderful if you could take a short minute and leave a review at www.freakyhealer.com, on Amazon.com, and Goodreads.com as soon as you can.

Your kind feedback helps other youngsters and parents find my books more easily, and be happy faster. Consider it a happy deed for the young people of the world. Thank you!

To find out more about my work and books check out:

www.freakyhealer.com

Jacqueline's Amazon Author Page

about the author

Jacqueline Pirtle is an internationally-renowned Mindful Happiness expert and the bestselling author of over 16 transformational personal growth books for adults and children.

She is a thought leader in the fields of mindfulness, happiness, energy work, energetic living and businessing, wholesome healing, and the teachings of one's soul.

Jacqueline has over 28 years of experience and has helped thousands of clients all over the world to discover their own happiness and how to live a conscious and mindfully aligned life filled with health, happiness, abundance, and success.

As the owner of *FreakyHealer* she has shared her solid teachings through her bestselling books, podcasts, sessions, workshops, courses and programs, talks and presentations with clients worldwide. She holds international degrees in holistic health and natural living and is a certified hypnotherapist for PTSD and Reiki Master.

Her highly effective healing work has been featured in print and online magazines, podcasts, radio shows, on TV, and in the documentaries *The Overly Emotional Child* by *Learning Success*, available on *Amazon Prime* and Hacking Happiness.

www.ingramcontent.com/pod-product-compliance
Lightning Source LLC
Chambersburg PA
CBHW061324120626
46546CB00007B/2664